SPECIALLY DESIGNED FOR AGES 5 TO 8

MONOPOLY
®
BRAND

JUNIOR

MR. MONOPOLY'S
AMUSEMENT PARK
A Math Adventure

ISBN 0-439-31792-4

12 11 10 9 8 7 6 5 4 3 2 1   1 2 3 4 5 6/0

Illustrated by Jim Talbot
Designed by Peter Koblish

Printed in the U.S.A.
First Scholastic printing, October 2001

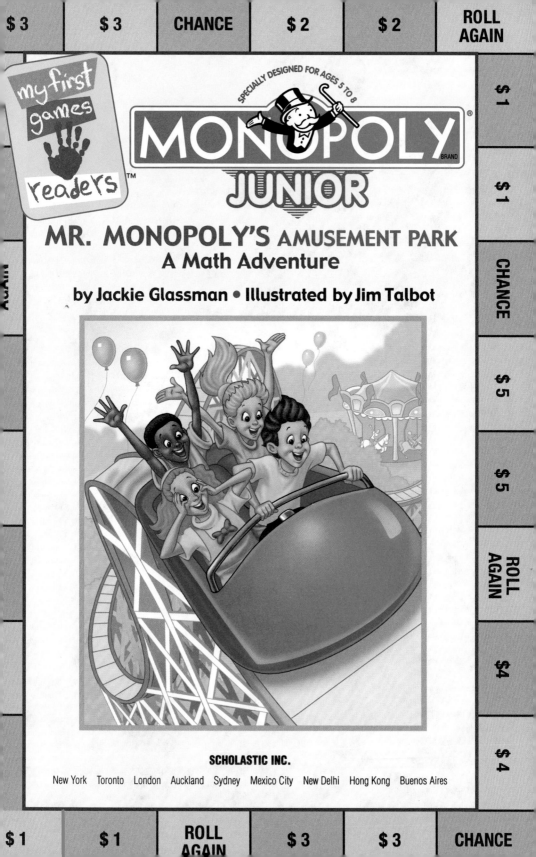

Welcome to Mr. Monopoly's Amusement Park.

Here is money for you and your friends.
Please keep track of what you spend.
Thirty dollars is a lot.
So, don't spend it in one spot.

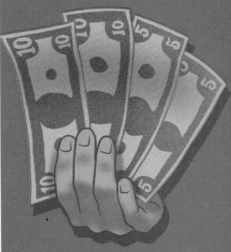

Extra Challenge

The kids got two ten-dollar bills and two five-dollar bills. Can you come up with three other ways to make thirty dollars?

A dollar each is a very good deal
For an extra-long ride on the Ferris wheel.
Up and down. Then 'round and 'round.
Our feet don't even touch the ground!

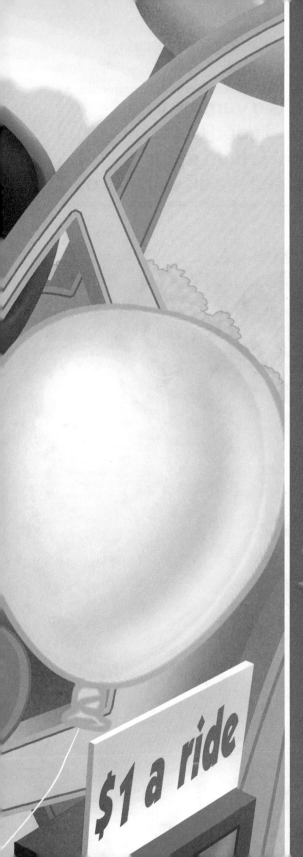

$1 a ride

Extra Challenge

If all four kids decide to ride on the Ferris wheel twice, how much will the ride cost them all?

Cotton candy is a yummy treat.
Pink, puffy, and good to eat.
This candy that is light as air
Is something that we all will share.

COTTON CANDY

COTTON CANDY for 75¢

COTTON CANDY
1 dollar each

Extra Challenge

What if the cotton candy costs seventy-five cents — then how much money would it cost in total for each child to have his or her own cotton candy?

Here we go down the water slide!
We paid fifty cents for each ride.
Up we go and down we splash.
Was it worth two dollars of our cash?

Waterslide 50¢

Extra Challenge

The children pay for the water slide with a five-dollar bill. How much change should they get back?

The two of us will go to Mars
While you guys ride the bumper cars.
When we're done, we will go
To the Hocus-pocus Magic Show!

BUMPER CARS

...I a ride

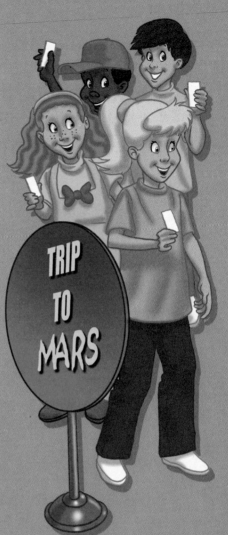

TRIP TO MARS

Extra Challenge

If all four kids decide to go on both rides, how much will it cost them all?

"Hocus-pocus!" the magician hollers.
In my cap, he finds two dollars.
"Abracadabra," he says to the crowd.
Then he vanishes in a cloud!

Extra Challenge

The kids decide to divide the two dollars evenly among themselves. How much money does each child get?

Video Arca

-1 dollar

Extra Challenge

The kids use a ten-dollar bill to pay for the arcade. But the cashier gives them back a five-dollar bill by accident. How much more does the cashier owe them?

It cost two dollars in all to go
To the super-duper puppet show.
We take our seats and the curtain rises.
Out pops a clown with silly surprises.

PUPPET SHOW
-50 CENTS-

PUPPET SHOW

Extra Challenge

If one of the kids decides not to go to the puppet show, how much will it cost them instead?

This ride is the most
Because in this house there lives a ghost.
The creepy monsters give us a chill,
But we still like the scary thrill.

Extra Challenge

If all four kids decide to go through the haunted house twice, how much will the ride cost?

The day has come to an end.
How much money did we spend?
How much do we have left?

Find the answer on the last page of this book.
Answers to the Extra Challenge questions are separate.

EXIT

The Ferris Wheel

It costs a total of four dollars for the children to ride on the Ferris wheel. If they pay with a ten-dollar bill, which of these pictures shows how much money they should get back?

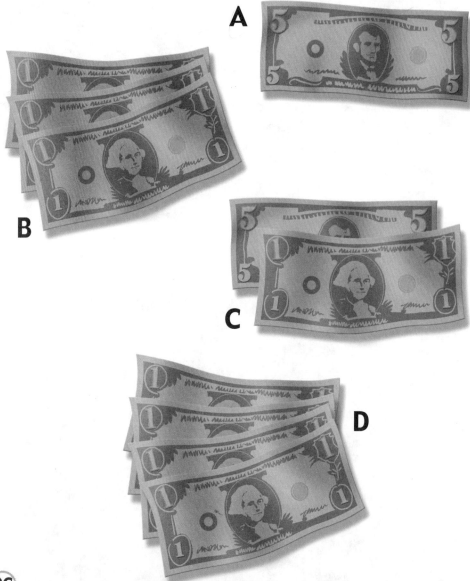

A

B

C

D

Fix the Mistake

The cotton candy costs a total of two dollars. The children pay with a five-dollar bill, but the man gives them back two dollars by mistake. How much more money does he owe them?

A

B

C

D

How Much?

The water slide costs fifty cents for each ride. How much does it cost for all four children to go down?

A

B

C

D

Hocus-pocus

After the magic show, the children have a total of eighteen dollars. Which picture shows how much they have?

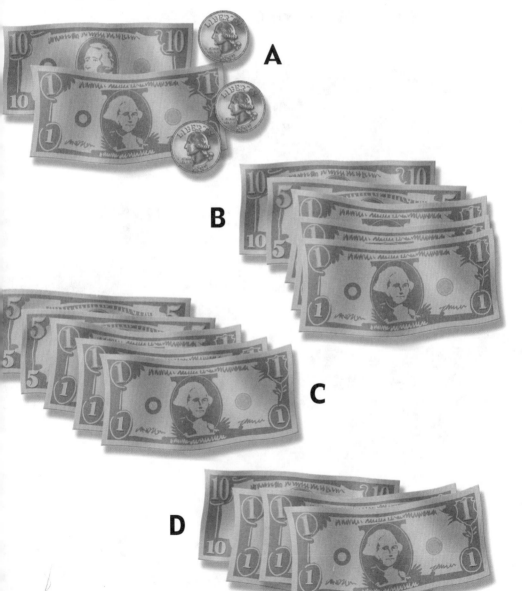

A

B

C

D

Spooky Math

The haunted house costs a total of eight dollars to enter. The children pay with a ten-dollar bill. All of the pictures show the correct amount of change except for which one?

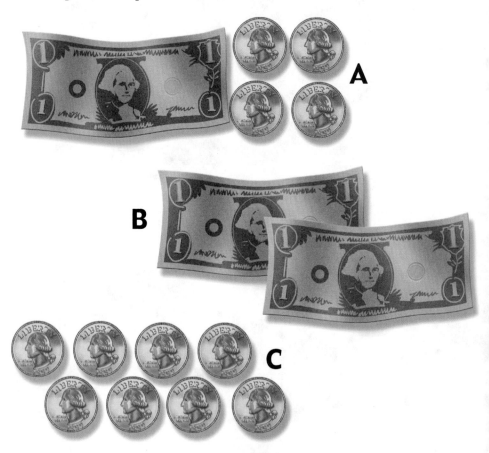

A

B

C

D

Balloons for Sale

At the end, the children have four dollars left. As they leave, they each buy a balloon for twenty-five cents each. After they buy the balloons, how much money will they have left?

A

B

C

D

Answers

Extra Challenge Answers

Page 7:   Answers may vary
Page 9: $8
Page 11: $3
Page 13: $3
Page 15: $12
Page 17:   50¢
Page 19: $1
Page 21: $1.50
Page 23: $16

At the end of the day, the
children have two dollars left.

The Ferris Wheel

"C"

Fix the Mistake

"B"

How Much?

"A"

Hocus-pocus

"B"

Spooky Math

"D"

Balloons for Sale

"A"